WORKBOOK ON

CUES

SkyBookz

Copyright – All Rights Reserved

Do not reproduce, transmit or store any part of this material without prior consent of the author or publisher.

Introduction

Every day we are communicating and whether we admit it or not, communication defines how people perceive and receive us. Our communication is grouped into three distinct parts; Nonverbal, Verbal and Vocal communication. However a large percentage of our communication is nonverbal and some people don't realize how powerful this type of communication model can project us. In this book, CUES the author Vanessa Van Edwards shares deep insights about our communication patterns and what makes us better communicators, how we fall in the four quadrant of the communication block. You will learn about the cues we send out during conversations, pitching and even during first dates with new people. The lessons in this book are great and very practicable if we are committed to learning and applying them. Finally, we can improve our communication skills if we choose to put in the work and hone the required skills to be better at our various communication approach.

Chapter One

Cue for Charisma

Questions

When you meet new people what are the first thing you look out for?

_____
_____
_____
_____
_____

Who has had the greatest impression on you?

_____
_____

Who is the most charismatic person you have met?

_____
_____

In your social networks, whose companionship do you enjoy the most?

_____

_____

Following your instincts and guts, how will you know if an acquaintance can be trusted and reliable?

_____

_____

_____

_____

_____

_____

How will you handle a workplace relationship with an unfriendly boss?

_____

_____

_____

_____

In your little way, how do you intend to improve the working atmosphere amongst your colleagues?

_____
_____
_____
_____
_____
_____
_____

When connecting with a total stranger what is the cues you look out for?

_____
_____
_____
_____
_____
_____

Chapter Two

How Cues Work

Questions

What are red flags?

_____
_____
_____
_____
_____

What will you consider to be red flags in a relationship for you?

_____
_____
_____
_____
_____
_____

When you see these red flags in people what is your response?

_____
_____
_____
_____
_____

As you strive to be an effective communicator, how will you strike the balance between warmth and competence?

_____
_____
_____
_____
_____

How will you know during a conversation that your partner is unhappy with you?

_____
_____
_____
_____
_____
_____

What nonverbal cues do you look out for when you meet people for the first time?

_____
_____
_____
_____
_____

How reliable are nonverbal cues in our communications with others?

_____
_____
_____

_____

_____

_____

On the scale of 1-10 how have you master the skill of mastering nonverbal cues?

_____

_____

Do you know how others perceive you in your social circle?

_____

Tell me how you think they do?

_____

_____

_____

_____

_____

Chapter Three

The Body Language of Leader

Questions

How do you intend to build trust among your friends?

_____
_____
_____
_____
_____

What and what will you do to improve your competence level?

_____
_____
_____
_____

_____

_____

What will you do to get the attention of anyone you are communicating with?

_____

_____

_____

_____

_____

How will you avoid the trap of sending wrong verbal cues?

_____

_____

_____

_____

_____

_____

What are your body postures when you are in a social setting?

_____
_____
_____

What does a firm handshake communicates to you?

_____
_____
_____

How will you know a confident and independent female/Male from her nonverbal cues?

_____
_____
_____
_____
_____

What can we do to stand out in a crowd of people during social networking?

_____
_____
_____
_____
_____

If the arms crossed the chest, what does it signify?

_____

What nonverbal cues do you use always?

_____
_____
_____
_____
_____

Chapter Four

The Wow Factor

Questions

What will you do to have a wow effect on the people you meet every day?

_____

_____

_____

_____

_____

What are the verbal and nonverbal cues you will use to achieve the experience?

_____

_____

_____

_____

Who is the person with the warmest aura you have ever met?

_____
_____

How can we dial up our warmth nonverbal cues?

_____
_____
_____
_____
_____

What will be your nonverbal cues to show your excitement about a partner?

_____
_____
_____
_____

What will be your nonverbal cues to show a dissatisfaction about an event going on in a social gathering?

_____
_____
_____

How would you differentiate between a real smile and a fake smile?

_____
_____
_____
_____
_____
_____

How do you feel when someone welcomes you with so much warmth?

_____
_____
_____

How can you tell if a person's action is signaling greenlight?

_____
_____
_____
_____
_____

What warm cues are you going to be using when you meet new people in life's journey?

_____
_____
_____
_____
_____

Chapter Five

How to Look Powerful

Questions

How will you know when someone is anxious?

_____

_____

_____

_____

_____

What do you think is the best sitting position when in a public space?

_____

_____

_____

When judging the overall body posture of a person how will you tell if they are confident?

_____

_____

_____

_____

_____

_____

How will you know a person's motives through their body?

_____

_____

_____

_____

_____

What makes you feel attracted to someone?

_____

_____

_____

_____

What is the best way to convey nonverbal information?

_____
_____
_____
_____
_____

Do you think gestures adds meaning to the verbal contents we hear?

_____

How would you explain a subject to someone with few words?

_____
_____
_____
_____
_____

Chapter Six

How to Spot a Bad Guy . . . and Not Be One Yourself

Questions

How can you decipher if one telling a lie or not?

_____
_____
_____
_____
_____
_____

What nonverbal cues do you notice once someone is lying?

_____
_____
_____
_____

What is the most notable bodily expression when someone is telling the truth?

_____
_____
_____

When recounting a negative event how do you feel?

_____
_____
_____
_____

What is your favorite self-soothing techniques?

_____
_____
_____
_____

If someone is self-soothing what does it mean?

_____
_____
_____
_____
_____

What should we do to stop been nervous in new environments?

_____
_____
_____
_____
_____

Whet self-gesture do you think can impact our charisma negatively?

_____
_____
_____

Chapter Seven

Sound Powerful

Questions.

What cues can we pick from people voices?

_____

_____

_____

Have you had situation where you liked someone just because of their voice?

_____

_____

Do you think its okay to judge people based on their voice?

_____

_____

How can we tell someone's emotional state from their voice?

_____
_____
_____
_____
_____

Have you had a situation where you heard someone speak and you out rightly disqualified them for been incompetent?

_____

How can we cultivate this charismatic presence when we speak?

_____
_____
_____
_____

What was your first speaking experience in front of an audience like?

_____
_____
_____
_____
_____

If you feel shaken on stage what is your first line of action?

_____
_____

What can we do to feel more confident when speaking?

_____
_____
_____
_____

Chapter Eight

Vocal Likability

Questions

What kind of speaker will you consider listening to when you are emotionally down?

_____

_____

In the face of crisis, how will judge if a speaker was empathetic and warmth?

_____

_____

_____

In what way can our personality affect our voicing?

_____

_____

_____

What can we do to sound more unique when we speak?

_____

_____

_____

_____

Have you ever picked a call and you could instantly feel the sadness of the caller?

_____

How would you know if a caller is happy or sad?

_____

_____

How can we sound warm and welcoming over a medium when the other person is not even seeing us?

_____

_____

_____

What are your favorite verbal warmth words?

_____

_____

_____

How can we build an instant warm rapport with people?

_____

_____

_____

_____

How can we improve our vocal feedbacks during conversations!

_____

_____

_____

Chapter Nine
How to Communicate with Charisma

Questions

How do you get people to buy into a new idea?

_____
_____
_____
_____
_____

When reading a new inbox message where do pay attention to the most?

_____

What are the adjectives that when people use them on you they brighten your mood?

_____
_____

When people connect with you on a deeper level how do you respond to their requests?

Does the level of connection with someone affect how you treat them?

If we audit your last five sent messages, how many warmth words can we find in those messages?

_____

_____

_____

How can we add positive verbal cues in our communications with people even in a professional environment?

_____

_____

_____

_____

_____

How do you say good bye in your native language?

_____

_____

How can we improve people's perception of us with verbal cues?

_____
_____
_____
_____
_____
_____

Do you think a perfect blend of nonverbal, vocal and verbal cues can makes us a better communicator?

_____
_____
_____

Chapter Ten
Creating a Powerful Visual Presence

Questions

What is your emotional association with Valentine's Day?

_____

_____

_____

_____

_____

What visual cues attracted you to your partner?

_____

_____

_____

What is the most expensive gift that you have been gifted?

What is the most expensive thing you have ever bought?

What verbal cues triggers the metaphor for an exquisite experience?

What visual metaphor triggers your sense of commitment?

What are the top 10 songs in your playlist?

_____

_____

_____

What visual cues attracted you to your favorite clothing designer?

_____

_____

_____

What visual cues reminds you of your favorite male actor?

_____

_____

_____

What cues influences most of your buying decision?

_____

_____

_____

Lessons Learned from the main book and this exercise.

_____

_____

_____

_____

_____

_____

_____

_____

_____

_____

_____

_____

_____

_____

_____

_____

_____

_____

_____

_____

Lessons Learned from the main book and this exercise.

Made in the USA
Monee, IL
23 October 2023